THE TEACHING CHURCH

THE
TEACHING
CHURCH

An Introduction
to Christian Education for
Parents and Teachers

Kendig Brubaker Cully

UNITED CHURCH PRESS
Philadelphia   Boston

To My Late Brother
William Bigler Cully, Jr.

Contents

Preface

THROUGHOUT THE WORLD hundreds and thousands of men and women are involved in the church's task of teaching the Christian faith. They teach as parents, whether they realize it or not; many teach formally in the church's schools. In the United States of America, Christian education is a principal concern of every branch of the church. To it is devoted a vast amount of time, energy, and money annually.

What the writer has sought to do in this brief introduction to Christian education for laymen—parents and teachers—is to help the readers to see their task in local situations and families as part and parcel of the world-wide ministry of the Christian church. It is hoped, too, that some who already have had experience in this educational concern of the church may benefit from a re-thinking of their responsibilities against the background presented in these pages.

For those who find this introduction whetting their appetite for further study in this field, the writer has appended a list of reading suggestions for the next step forward.

KENDIG BRUBAKER CULLY

Evanston, Illinois

1:

Why
The Church
Teaches

As THE LONG history of the Christian church clearly shows, many views have been held concerning the nature of the church. One of the great achievements of ecumenical discussions in recent decades has been the frank facing of different attitudes and practices. Instead of staying separately in their respective corners, Christians have been learning more and more to sit down in friendly conversation. They are learning to explain to one another how they think and feel about such basic questions as the place of the Bible, the understanding of the sacraments, the form and spirit of worship, and the relationship of Christian doctrine to the pressing social problems of the world. They have discovered that often they share much more than they had earlier realized, and that they have much to learn from one another as well as to give to one another. Perhaps even more significant than the conversations themselves are the occasions in which Christians of diverse traditions have been able

9

to kneel down and pray together to their common heavenly Father. In such times of prayer they have experienced the reality of belonging together in spite of, or even because of, their different interpretations.

While this ecumenical rediscovery of essential unity in Jesus Christ has been taking place, Christians of every communion have continued to pursue the tasks to which they have felt themselves called by God. They have provided opportunities for their people's worship; they have carefully arranged the internal organization of their churches' life and work; they have established the various agencies and institutions which have seemed desirable or necessary for the carrying on of Christian purposes.

One of the basic unchanging tasks is the proclamation of the gospel. To be sure, the gospel itself has been variously defined and understood; but all communions have sought to put into effect Jesus' commandment that the disciples should go into all the world, preaching the gospel to mankind everywhere. Some churches have been more zealous for evangelistic outreach than others. Some churches have felt that their chief duty was to proclaim the gospel within their own national boundaries, to people of their own race, language, and customs. Others have felt that the world as a whole was their parish and that missionary work in far places was just as important as the work in their own nations. In one way or another, every body of Christians has felt in some measure the burden it has to bear in proclaiming the good news of the redemption of the world by God in Jesus Christ.

Thus the church has as its first task the confronting of men, women, and children with the saving knowledge of God who has come into the world with power and love in Christ. In Christ the New Being has been brought into existence by God. Through faith all of us can share now in the joyous wonder of his mighty acts for our redemption. The first task of the church, then, is to preach this good news and to help people to understand that this is something for them to receive as the answer to their loneliness, their estrangement, and their sin. The church should not seek to "frighten" people into salvation. Rather, it should tell lovingly and winsomely the mighty faith that it has received as a free gift from God, which it holds as a treasure to share with all who will accept.

The result of the proclamation of the gospel is the continual growth and renewal of the church by the coming of new believers into it. This is not to be thought of in terms of increase in numbers alone. There will be times in history when the church is very large in numbers; at other times only a few will seem to hear the message and to respond to it. But the church can never be content to stand still. Being the bearer of this gospel means that the church's members will ever be seeking others to join them in Christian fellowship.

Living in "fellowship" is the second great characteristic of the Christian church. Those who respond to the Word are not simply individuals who have been privileged to receive the gift of God's love and forgiveness. They are blessed as individuals, to be sure. But they are also drawn into an intimate company of those who to-

gether confess the faith that they have received. This
is the church, "the blessed company of all faithful people." Those who receive such a faith share it with others.
They are, all together, the ones who recognize that
Christ died for them. His living presence is with them
to sustain and to direct them. This is the meaning of the
phrase, "the Body of Christ." Every member of the
fellowship recognizes that all the others are sharers in
the abundant mercy of Christ; and they express their
fellowship in those various actions which Christ himself ordained as the means by which the special nature
of this fellowship was to be set forth. They enter the
church through baptism. They gather together in the
celebration of the Lord's Supper, wherein by the breaking of bread and the drinking of the cup they are constantly reminded of his presence with them. They gather
for prayer and praise, especially on Sundays, which have
become for them the weekly reminder of the first Easter.
They join in the Lord's Prayer and other words used
everywhere throughout the whole church. These unite
them with one another and with Christ. They read one
common book, the Bible, which is the written record
of the encounter of God with men, and it becomes
through faith a living word for them. In this fellowship
they develop a common concern for one another's problems, strengthen one another's faith, and find a warm,
vibrant center for their human relationships on earth.

No person is automatically a Christian. He is brought
into Christian knowledge either through having been
born into a Christian family that nurtures his spiritual
growth or through conversion as an adult. In either case,

his growth as a Christian is influenced by the surroundings and the atmosphere into which he is drawn by his association with the witnessing, worshiping community of the church. Various members of the church will manifest different degrees of understanding and of devotion, since individual Christians are not identical with one another. The Christian experience of no one Christian is exactly the same as that of any other Christian. Each brings with him his own personality and temperament, his particular physical and social inheritance, and his own intellectual points of view.

The church therefore must provide means through which these many and varied kinds of people, who come into its sphere of influence, can grow, each according to his own needs and talents, into a fully developed Christian life. Thus arises the need for the church to teach. The mere fact of being an organized society makes it necessary for the church to accept the responsibility of being a teaching body. Every organized group in society provides teaching for its members, and in this respect the church can be no different from any other group. For every group in society is organized with a view to the fulfillment of some purpose, which it claims to understand; and only those members who share in the understanding of its purpose and who act in accordance with its aims can be counted on to help it in the fulfillment of what it believes to be its task.

Unlike other groups in society, however, the church feels that it has a meaning for the whole world of men. That is, the church does not regard itself as merely another competing institution among many. It is *the* society. It is first of all called into being by God as a means by which his eternal will can be carried out. It is sustained not merely by purposes worked out in committees but by the living presence of its Lord and Savior. What it must teach, therefore, is determined by its spiritual origin and destiny. To put it another way, the teaching ministry of the church is not an end in itself. Its teaching is based on the proclamation of the gospel. The subject matter, its curriculum, is derived from this gospel.

Preaching—proclaiming the gospel—is not the same as teaching, but it is the foundation of teaching. When people have responded to the proclamation, then teaching must follow. It is not enough for a man to learn the "bare facts." These must be explained until he consciously understands them and until they are related to the demands of Christ on the whole of his life. This is especially true of Christian teaching, for the Christian faith embraces not merely a small segment of human life but the whole of life. One does not become a Christian simply through an exercise of the will, or by an act of mental choice, or by subscribing to a set of propositions laid down in a creed. One becomes a Christian when the whole of one's existence is turned in faith toward Christ. The Christian religion therefore will affect the whole of one's existence in every part. Ideas, feelings, moral standards, social behavior, and physical expression will all be involved. The whole range of human experience will come to be interpreted differently by reason of one's faith. For this reason Christian teaching will have to take into consideration the entire range of human experience and learning as well as the distinctively Christian "facts." Those who come into the church live also in the world. If they are to be mature Christians, they will need to see the relationships between the faith they profess and the life they live in the workaday world.

This has been true throughout the centuries of the church's existence. It was evident in Jesus' manner of dealing with grave questions of practical daily life. For example, he saw that men need to be shown the right relationship between loyalty to God and loyalty to the state. He said, "Render to Caesar the things that are Caesar's, and to God the things that are God's" (Mark 12:17). Christians living in the modern world—or in any period of history—have to do some serious studying and thinking if they are to understand how that relationship applies in their own country and their own situation, and how to act according to it. The Christian has no business imagining that the duties he has to perform as a citizen have nothing to do with his duties as a Christian. He will have to do some earnest studying, both of the things pertaining to Caesar and those pertaining to God. Faith does not set us free from the need for secular knowledge; it must be related to it at all points along the line.

It is for such reasons that the church must teach. It must first of all teach its own faith, doctrine, and practices in order that its people may have a reason for the faith that is in them. This means that its curriculum will be centered in the Bible, in the thinking of the first theologians of the church (the church fathers of East and West), and in the history of the church, including the development of creeds, sacraments, and worship. Each communion will of course stress its own particular views of the faith; but increasingly, in the light of ecumenical discussion, it will try to appreciate and to treat fairly the traditions of other churches, with which at many points it is in agreement. At all times the church will seek to stress those greatest truths which are shared by all Christians, though different interpretations of them in detail may be given by the various churches. When the response of faith is supplemented and accompanied by careful teaching, the church will be making sure that its people have a faith that is supported by knowledge; that is, a faith that is related to the foundations on which the church is built.

At this point, however, we must indicate something that may prove a great hindrance to the kind of teaching which is truly based on the gospel itself. We might refer to this as "false objectivity." Sometimes a doctrine can be taught in such a way that it becomes a very wooden and lifeless thing. Of course we must include as part of our teaching, ideas *about* various aspects of the Christian religion: the teaching of Jesus, the way in which the apostle Paul made his missionary journeys, the narratives of the Old Testament, the reasons for the branching of the church into Eastern and Western, and the varieties of Protestant Christianity at the time of the Reformation and subsequently. It is one thing to learn *about* an idea, but it is another thing to make the idea a part of ourselves so that we genuinely share in the reality that the idea represents. The church's best teaching has always used a knowledge of the facts as a springboard for fuller participation in the reality about which the facts give evidence. Take such a tremendous matter as the doctrine of the Holy Spirit. It would perhaps be possible for pupils to learn many things about that doctrine, yet fail in the end to stand in the presence of the mystery which that doctrine discloses; to know a great many things *about* the Holy Spirit, and yet to fail absolutely to know *him*.

This, then, is the goal that the church should set before itself: to teach so that in the very process of learning, the members of the church will be entering ever more fully and richly into a living experience of the realities that they are studying. Only thus can the church be sure that its members will become genuinely practicing Christians, in contrast to those theoretically trained adherents who know all about the faith but do not really know it from within.

We have said that the teaching of the church must be based on the proclamation of the gospel. It is also to be remembered that the teaching takes place within the fellowship of the church itself. The really vital teaching church is one in which the life of the congregation is genuine and the Holy Spirit is a reality admitted into the daily life of the people. Even if the general life of a congregation has become dull and rigid, it can still perform a certain limited ministry, provided that a few deeply Christian souls remain alert and working within it. Such is the nature of human relationships, however, that a dynamic enthusiasm quickly passes from one spirit to another. If all the members of a congregation maintain an awareness of their spiritual calling and destiny, and live a common life in which Christian worship and work are shared devoutly and regularly by many, the chances are much higher that all who come within the influence of that congregation will be impelled to know and understand the full reality of the faith that they profess. They will be simultaneously a teaching and a learning church.

Every Christian is a teacher in the sense that by his attitudes and example he is influencing others. And every Christian is a learner in the sense that he is always acquiring from his assocation with others in the church some deeper insight, some new grasp of holy truth. This is a very real aspect of the functioning of the fellowship. Without consciously setting itself up to be a school in the formal sense, the fellowship is inevitably a school in the sense that teaching and learning are always going forward hand in hand. At times the church will deliberately set up schools in the formal sense. But only to the extent that those schools manifest in themselves the quality of mutual teaching and learning can they themselves become adequate agencies of Christian education.

In summary, then, we can say these things:

1. The church's primary function is to proclaim the gospel.

2. The relationship of Christians to one another in the church is expressed in the fellowship wherein Christ is present among his own, "the Body of Christ."

3. Christians live also in the daily workaday world, and the church's teaching must relate the gospel to the demands and pursuits that make up the general body of experience of Christians living in the world.

4. The church must make sure that through its teaching, its members learn the facts about their religion. But these facts need to be interpreted in such a way as to lead to inward personal sharing in the spiritual realities that lie behind the facts.

5. The church as a fellowship is made up of those who are mutually teaching one another and learning from one another.

Why does the church teach? The church teaches because it cannot help doing so if it is going to be true to its own foundations in the living gospel. The church teaches in order that a full and joyous faith may characterize its present generation and be handed on, by the grace of God, to its future members.

2:

In
Each
Country

IF THE FAITH is to be interpreted vitally to its present members and handed on to coming generations, the church is bound to teach. However, the church's teaching must of necessity be carried on under the circumstances that exist in particular times and places.

On the one hand, the Christian community is worldwide, international, and universal in terms of the fundamental allegiance that Christians offer to God through Christ. The symbols of word and action used in worship and devotion are recognizable across the boundary lines of nations. This is abundantly evident on those occasions when worldwide conferences of churchmen are held, as in the assemblies of the World Council of Churches. The text of the ritual for worship is usually made available in several languages; but there has been no experience of confusion even when worshipers repeat the phrases of the Lord's Prayer, each in his own tongue, or sing the stanzas of hymns together in a wide variety of languages. Unlike the Roman Catholics, who use

Latin as a *lingua franca* for worship, Protestants have long insisted that if Christians are to take an intelligent part in worship, it is essential that every man should have the opportunity to worship in the language he ordinarily speaks at home. Yet it has been demonstrated many times that the symbols of worship speak in and through themselves, especially in baptism and the Lord's Supper, regardless of the language barrier between those of different races.

However, churches work in specific countries and in particular situations. The language one speaks is so intimately a part of human intercourse that most men like to work and worship with those to whom they are linked by the use of a common language. Thus it is possible to find English-speaking congregations on the continent of Europe and in Latin America; Greek-speaking congregations in North America; Chinese-speaking congregations in Indonesia, and so forth. The need for the provision of worship in a number of different languages in countries to which immigrants have gone in large numbers diminishes as second- and third-generation settlers acquire the tongue of their new country. This is illustrated by the gradual adoption of English by many American congregations which in earlier times had used German or one of the Scandinavian languages. As immigrants in America became assimilated into the new culture, their former language was used less and less. This pattern is repeating itself in Canada, in Australia, and in other newly settled areas today.

In most Western countries the majority of Christians, of course, are likely to use one major language (or two

in the few bilingual countries, and four in Switzerland).
The problem of language communication is therefore
comparatively simple. The means of mass communication—newspapers, books, radio, television—are available
for the transmission of religion as well as for other kinds
of human experience. The church has contributed
notably to the spread of literacy in countries where until
recent years there have always been large numbers of
persons unable to read. What has led the church to in-
sist so much on the teaching of reading is that Christianity is the religion of a Book; Christians are expected
to be able to read the Bible. The gospel can be received
in its fullness only among those who personally have
access to the message of the Bible. A new Christian attracted by the call of faith into the life of a congregation
will want to share fully and completely in its life; and
the use of the language that he knows best will be the
bridge on which he and his new-found friends in Christ
can consider together the shared realities of faith.

The life of a church in a particular country will be influenced in more ways than by the matter of language.
The climate will determine to a large extent the archi-
tectural forms used for church buildings. In the now-
passed or nearly passed period when missionary work in
Africa and the East was directed from Western countries, many of the missionaries, almost without knowing
it, thought of the Christian religion as identified with
certain forms to which they had been accustomed at
home. The result was the erection of church structures
that more nearly resembled what they had known in
England, the United States of America, or Germany

than anything to be seen in the new countries where they had made their homes. Similarly, habits pertaining to such matters as dress, food, and music, with which the missionaries had been familiar in their home countries, were often exported along with the articles of faith.

As we look back, some of these tendencies seem to have been naive and, unfortunately, related to a time during which the West was able to dominate the East. But at least sometimes the result was to help new Christians from the start to understand that the church is a worldwide body that does not belong to either East or West. Christianity in its essence is worldwide; if it has to express itself in particular forms, it is desirable that Christians of every country should recognize a kind of oneness with one another, even in such minor matters as having in common certain kinds of architecture and certain types of music. Fortunately, in recent decades, the quick forms of communication and travel have permitted Christians in almost every country to know at least something of national forms of expression elsewhere. A case in point was the international hymnal published by the World's Student Christian Federation and used at the Evanston Assembly of the World Council of Churches, *Cantate Domino*. This contained fine hymns from many nations. Many volumes of collected prayers and religious paintings from many countries of the world have been published in various languages. The religious press helps to develop a worldwide viewpoint; the principal journals of all the churches contain articles on many phases of Christian life and culture throughout the world.

The principle emerging seems not to be the reduction

of Christian life to one uniform level throughout the world. Rather, each country by its own national genius and character can give expression to the common life in Christ in such manner as to enrich all others who may come into contact with it.

In just the same way, in its educational work the church will of necessity vary from country to country in its approaches, philosophy, and methods. There are certain well-tested avenues for Christian educational work that have come to have value for churches everywhere. In its use of any method, and in its choice of emphases, each church should seek to base its approach on its own special needs, facilities, and resources, as these are related to the country in which it is placed and the culture in the midst of which it has to work.

An examination of the history of each country will show how many types of relationship between organized religion and the state have existed across the years.

In Europe it was the church that took the initiative in providing education for children in schools that in earlier days were controlled by the clergy. The formation of schools, which at first were available in the main to boys who were being trained for the priesthood, grew out of the church's concern to provide for itself an educated leadership. Since the church had been first in providing educational opportunities, what happened in most countries was that even when the state became concerned about educating its citizens, the administration of education and the curriculum were still left in the hands of the clergy. This continued even after the Reformation.

However, the rise of national states altered the situation considerably. The spread of the desire for education among ever larger numbers of people made it impossible for the church to meet all the needs, and this led the state to take over more and more of the financial responsibility. As the national governments became more powerful, they desired to regulate and even to operate the schools that they were supporting financially. By the end of the eighteenth century and the beginning of the nineteenth century, this was already true in many countries: education was passing into the hands of the state. In many cases the church continued to operate schools, but now for the most part there was some state control.

The Yearbook of Education (London, 1951) gives a useful description of the five principal categories of state-church relationship with regard to education as it currently exists in various parts of the world.

1. Situations in which the majority of the population adhere to a single church or religion, and where there are few hostile to it. Examples are Portugal, the Irish Republic (Roman Catholic), Sweden (Lutheran), and Pakistan (Islam).

2. Countries where only one denomination has a large number of adherents, but where its control is repudiated by many citizens. Examples are France and Belgium, where a considerable number of people prefer to be considered freethinkers, humanists, agnostics, or otherwise religiously unrelated.

3. Countries where several religious denominations are found, none being really dominant and none strongly objected to. Examples are the United States of America, Australia, Canada, and the Netherlands.

4. Countries of various religious complexions where the state has established an educational monopoly. Examples are the U.S.S.R. and Communist China.

5. Countries where a special problem exists, such as schools maintained by foreign authorities or by minority communities within the state. Examples are some colonial and nonself-governing territories; mission schools or government schools, such as French schools in Iran and Afghanistan, or Chinese schools in Malaya, Indonesia, and Borneo.

This diversified situation produces many varieties of the control of education. In Spain, for example, there is Roman Catholic supremacy and no freedom of education for those who are not Roman Catholics. In Canada, the government both subsidizes schools that are operated by churches and conducts state-operated schools. In England and Wales there is provided a dual control of certain schools, in which both church and state share. In the Irish Republic policies are determined by councils of parents. In the United States of America, state schools are the only ones legally permitted to receive money from public treasuries; if certain churches wish to conduct schools of their own, they must themselves raise all the money that is required.

We are not concerned here to go into detail regarding these many varieties of state-church relations in education. These varieties are cited in order to make clear how difficult it is to make any general statements about Christian education. What is true in one country may be entirely untrue in another.

When a church endeavors to determine what its responsibility is in education, it must do so in the light of the prevailing laws and traditions of the country where it does its principal work. If it has missionary work overseas and wishes to make education a part of that work, then the way in which that work can be carried out will be determined by the laws and traditions of the country where the mission is established. The situation in a foreign country may be entirely different from that in the church's native land. This is not to say that a church need regard the law and tradition of its own country as final and unchangeable. Like other organized groups in society, a church may find it to be part of its duty to seek to educate public opinion and in certain matters to secure a change of the law; but this is a long process, and one that must be engaged in with due respect to the feelings and rights of others.

Obviously, the church's task in education will vary with the kind of national situation that provides the context within which it must operate. There are some countries where the state is anti-Christian and where no influence on educational policies is possible. Sometimes the state in such cases is openly resistant to public Christian teaching of any kind; then the church's primary work must be with its own members, and that, often, done quietly without drawing any public attention to what it is doing. In such countries the privilege of giving Christian teaching has to be bought at a very high price, and persecution of those who practice it has not been unknown.

Other countries publicly take the position that for the sake of religious liberty no formal religious instruction is permissible in the schools, although there is complete freedom for the churches to do whatever public teaching they desire. In such countries the churches cannot expect financial assistance from the state. Nor can there be any sectarian teaching of religion in the public schools. Yet the churches are at perfect liberty to arrange for religious instruction in any form they like—either in schools which they found and carry on and finance themselves, or within the life of the religious community itself. It is usually in such countries that the churches have been led of necessity to great resourcefulness in devising various educational means which will guarantee that their people will be properly educated as Christians.

In some countries, notably in Germany, Great Britain, and the Scandinavian nations, the schools are in part at least under the control of the state and are supported from the public taxes. Religion is integrally included as a part of the curriculum. In some cases the religion taught is that of an established church; in others, the religious instruction must be done on a basis mutually agreeable to the cooperating churches. But in any event, it is taken for granted by the state that the religion in which the children will be instructed is the Christian religion, unless the parents (for example, Jewish parents) particularly desire it otherwise. In such cases individual congregations may assume that the formal, objective, factual religious instruction will be done in the state schools; then special teaching in the life and worship of the church will be the responsibility of the parish, which will carry it out with greater or less efficiency according to its inclination.

The different modes of approach to the matter of education in various countries might lead one to the impression that all is chaos, that there is nothing in common across international boundaries with regard to educational principles and methods. This, however, would be a false conclusion. There is much more in common than is evident on the basis of first impressions. Although the church must adjust its approach to the national tradition in which it finds itself, certain things belong to the church's teaching task in all countries and in every generation.

1. The subject matter of the faith is the same everywhere in regard to its basic ingredients. The Bible must be taught. Christians must be made reasonably conversant with the history of the traditions of the church, beliefs must be examined, and Christian moral principles explored.

2. Christian education will have to embrace the needs of the same kinds of members in every land. There will be the newly baptized; there will be the core of faithful people who need to penetrate ever more deeply into the realities which they find in the faith; there will be the lapsed, the careless, and the indifferent parishioners. All these must be the concern of the church, which must try to fit its educational program to their many and varying needs.

3. In all countries the church faces the challenge produced by secularistic and communistic ideologies. No country is in the position of having the Christian religion so deeply entrenched at the heart of its national life that assaults from without cannot avail. Christians of all coun-

tries today have discovered that the teaching ministry of the church increases in importance with every attack against religion from any secularist source. Parents and teachers of the very young as well as of college or university students are well aware of the ways in which these nonreligious influences manifest themselves. Much modern education is based on scientific and materialistic foundations. Although there need be no conflict between the scientific viewpoint and the Christian faith, we of the church have not always been able to make a strong enough impression on our youth to counteract a tendency for the scientific outlook to engulf the whole approach of our children to life. Does the Bible seem out of date to young people getting used to laboratory techniques that can launch sputniks into outer space? Does prayer seem quaintly pious to those who have been taught to put their trust in human reason to solve almost every problem? Do the sacraments speak meaningfully to a generation that prefers to handle things rather than symbols? In every country Christians must learn how to interpret the faith to the young in such a manner that they will have a right approach to faith instead of thinking of faith as an outmoded alternative to the approaches they are taught in school.

4. Human beings are essentially the same in all countries and all cultures. The human situation is the same: estrangement from God until the New Being in Christ comes into our lives to relate us to his holy and eternal purposes. This is revealed to us now in joy and glory and power as we respond in faith to Jesus Christ. All who respond to Christ, whether few or many, will ask new

questions because of what he has done for them; old answers to old questions will no longer suffice to meet their needs. The church in all times and places must encourage Christians both to ask the ever-new questions inspired by faith and to seek the ever-renewed answers, freshly interpreted in each generation, as these are required by Christians living in the midst of a changing and complex world. It is the same in this respect whether one is a citizen of Europe or the Orient, where national destinies have ancient roots, or a citizen of one of the newest self-governing democracies in Africa. The formulations will vary, but the process will be the same.

5. In every country Christians face today, as they have from the first century on, the question as to what extent non-Christian traditions and practices can be incorporated into the life of the Christian community without jeopardizing the purity of the faith. The apostle Paul had to deal with questions like this when he learned that some Christians were eating meat which had first been sacrificed to pagan gods. Those who live and work in cultures that have only recently been receiving the impact of Christianity often have to face questions such as these: What shall a new Christian do concerning his several wives, in view of the church's teaching on monogamous marriage? How shall a new Christian act toward members of his family who disapprove of his taking the step into baptism? Does a new Christian have to forsake all attachment to the scriptures of another religion in which he was nurtured as a child? Theologians vary in their interpretation of matters like these; but in the practical educational tasks of the church, definite views must

be adopted and decisions made. Here, too, it would be impossible to state a general rule with universal binding power, nor dare the Christians of one country presume to dictate to fellow Christians in a different culture precise solutions for the problems which are peculiarly theirs.

3:

For

All

Ages

CHRISTIAN EDUCATION involves both practice and philosophy (theory). By philosophy is meant the effort made by experts to work out certain basic principles of education and of teaching method, by which the church may be guided in its practical educational efforts. The philosopher, unlike the practitioner, is not principally concerned with the way various methods work. He is interested in thinking through basic aims and goals, leaving the practical working out of details to the educators—the teachers, administrators, and pastors.

If we look at the history of Christian education from the time of the church fathers down to the present day, we find that there are two aspects that, with greater or less emphasis, always have to be borne in mind.

First, there is the institutional angle. This pertains to the transmission of the faith from generation to generation; to the manner in which the Christian community, the church, assures its own continuity, or regards itself as the vehicle through which the Holy Spirit continues to function in the realm of the New Being, the kingdom of God. This institutional aspect of education is important; it does not simply provide for the self-preservation of a valued order of things; it demands that the church should again and again think through its aim and purposes in terms of what the church itself is. Is the church the same as the surrounding culture? Few would argue that it is, or ought to be; yet some have insisted that the church's function is to transform the kingdoms of men into the kingdom of God. On the other hand, is the church a thing entirely apart from the surrounding culture? Should the Christian community seek to be different in every way from its environment, calling its people out of the world in order that they may live in a reality of an entirely different kind? Some bodies of Christians in various periods of the church's history have taken this view. It is typified in the ascetic tendency to withdraw from the active existence into the contemplative life of the monastery. Or it can be seen in the views of some Christian bodies which set up severe rules for their members, refusing them permission to indulge in many of the forms of social expression in which "the worldly" engage.

Any philosophy of Christian education will have to be developed on the basis of a carefully thought out understanding of what the nature of the church itself is in relation to the world.

A second aspect, which confronts us in every attempt to understand the basic principles of Christian education, pertains to the attitude of the church toward individuals. What do we mean by the term persons, and what is the place of persons in the scheme of things? Why should individuals be singled out for special attention in the church? How are individuals related to one another in the Christian community? Is there a special "Christian" relationship, different from those that prevail in secular communities?

There is general agreement among thinkers in this field that Christianity values the individual highly not simply for himself but because he is the creation of God. In the realm of the New Being which Jesus Christ brought into existence, persons are valued more highly than things. Things must never be confused with persons. If persons are treated as if they were things, they are made subject to manipulation by other men for selfish ends, or they are made subservient to any institution. This involves a denial of the reality of the God by whom they were made. The church itself is a community of *persons*; it can never fulfill its true destiny simply by becoming a large and powerful institution.

The church must always be an institution; but it is so only in order to make possible and to promote that fellowship of persons held together by love, which must characterize the church when it is truly the Body of Christ.

Thus the philosopher of Christian education will ever seek to bring together in fruitful union these two aspects of the task—the life of the Christian community as a whole and the growth of persons one by one.

A term which has been widely used across the years is appropriate to describe that aspect of the process which refers to individual growth. This phrase is "Christian nurture." This refers to the process of providing nourishment for the personality, in the manner that a good gardener seeks to surround a young plant with good and fertile soil and seeks to water it so that it will become what it can become under right circumstances favoring growth. There are two major areas in which we can think of religious education. One area puts the emphasis on the transmission of objective facts about the religious heritage to the child. This rather implies putting something into the child "from outside." We have seen above that a fact is useful for Christian growth only when it leads to fuller and inward sharing in the reality which the fact represents. The other area is that in which stress is placed upon the individual's personal growth and self-discovery. When this method is followed, the church does not so much seek to fill the child's mind with lessons and doctrines as it does to surround him with helpful suggestions and aids, so that he himself will discover the meaning of the faith as he grows in age and understanding. This may be described as encouraging growth "from within."

There does not seem to be any reason why these two areas should be set over against each other, as though the one in some way contradicted the other. Certainly few who stress the need for persons to learn the facts about the Christian religion would ever urge that the mastery of the facts alone is an end in itself; rather, these facts are to be learned to the end that personalities may be built up in Christ. Nor does the argument that persons need to discover the meanings of faith in terms of their personal growth imply that individuals can become

Christians purely in terms of their individual self-development, isolated from others. Growth in personal religious insight means that the church, too, must become part of the experience of the individual, as he comes to a fuller understanding of the faith; for Christian growth must always be in terms of the fellowship.

Certainly all churches have become increasingly aware in recent decades that every single person who enters into the church's life stands in need of Christian nurture throughout the whole of his life. This is not a task directed only toward the children of believers, or toward other children who for various reasons are brought into contact with the organized church. Nor is it primarily a question of Christian youth movements, or of work with the mature in years. To be sure, all these groups require all the specialized program and activities, suitable to their various ages, which the church can devise. Yet none should be emphasized to the neglect of the others.

Many congregations have failed to understand that it is the duty of the church to meet the needs of those of all ages within its fellowship. Some churches get the reputation in their community of being "old folks' churches" or "churches bulging to the seams with young people." The implication of such descriptions is that some age groups are being overlooked because of an unbalanced concentration of interest on a "specialty." One of the most enriching aspects of the fellowship's life is the opportunity given to people of many ages to work and worship with those of other groups.

The family analogy is appropriate here. The church is like a large family. There will be the older people, many of them serenely wise because of the experiences the years have brought them. In them the prayer has been truly answered, that as they grow in age they might also grow in the knowledge and love of God and of his truth. There will be people at the height of their productive and creative years, busy and active in labor, business, or professional life, bringing their intensive powers into the total life of the parish. The young married couples, starting to assume ever larger responsibilities and deeply concerned over the life of their young children, can contribute enthusiasm and energy to the life of the congregation. They can also offer a constant reminder through their children that the church is at all times confronted with a new generation, one that will present it with fresh demands and problems for teaching. Adolescents and older unmarried youth, confronted with the countless challenges of our modern culture, are weighing alternatives, beginning to choose their careers and making plans for getting married, and deciding just what part religion is going to play in their lives. An active youth program is indispensable if Christianity is to capture the loyalty of these young people, and if their talents are to be invested in the enterprises of the kingdom of God. The small children are the cradle of the church, a reminder constantly that God's purposes include the youngest as well as the oldest members of the community. From birth on, these children of the believers are the responsibility of the whole church and not only of the parents and godparents. It is no accident that the baptismal ritual of many churches includes a commendation of newly baptized babies to the care of Christ's flock.

There is a growing tendency to bring whole families into the worshiping congregation instead of keeping the children separate until they are old enough to attend services with some reasonable hope of their being able to understand what is going on. Usually when this family view of worship is accepted, the very young children are brought into the service for only a part of the hour, perhaps leaving before the sermon to go to their own groups. By the time they are old enough to be fully confirmed members of the congregation, there is every reason to hope that the habit of worship will be so firmly developed in them that they will wish to carry out the duty of adults in attending throughout the whole worship period.

The regular Sunday worship will be the central point of vitality in the church. From this should flow the spiritual energies that will make all auxiliary activities of the parish relevant and strong. It is evident that the Christian quality of classes, clubs, and groups will be maintained only if these are under the leadership of people who love the Father's house and worship regularly with the faithful.

At the same time, it has been the experience of most churches that the various age groups and sexes have different needs and enjoy working together as groups for the planning of program and activities adapted to meet their own inclinations or needs. Thus children six to eight years old are generally happier when brought together in a group with children of their own age than they are with children of a somewhat older age. The unmarried young adults (eighteen to twenty-five years old, for ex-

ample) are more likely to enjoy certain conversations and
activities with others of their own age and unmarried
state than they would being mixed in with young married adults.

Here, then, is the foundation of planning in the
church: the emotional needs of the different ages vary,
and wise planning will attempt to meet them all. Need-
less to say, what is or can be done along these lines will
vary from congregation to congregation. A very small
church with only a few persons in each age group and a
very large church with multitudes of people will naturally
vary a great deal in the possibilities of action open to
each.

One question that always arises is whether the arrange-
ment of groups for study, work, and activity should
usually be planned to separate the sexes or planned in
ways that bring them together. Traditions vary in this
respect from Germany, for example, where the tendency
is for most church clubs, even of older young people, to
be segregated, except for occasional joint activities, to
the United States of America, where coeducation is cus-
tomary in the public schools as well as in churches from
the earliest ages onward. Men and women have traditionally done some things separately in the church, as is
evident from the fact that so many churches have separate organizations for men and for women. On the other
hand, a very interesting new development in a number
of churches has been the rise of activities in which young
married couples take part together. It is possible that
when married men and women work together in the
church for a longer period of time, and are joined also by

unmarried people of about the same age, there will be a
tendency toward less segregation of the sexes. It is evident, after all, that men and women have taken part in
worship together for many centuries, though there has
been a tendency for them to carry on their other activities through separate organizations.

One other development should be noted: the rise of
special work among the older members of the church.
Sometimes the oldest parishioners are forgotten or
neglected, not deliberately but because there are so many
other things to do and because so many of the old
friends of their earlier years are gone. The increasing life
expectancy of the human family, due to modern advances
in medicine and public health, means that people everywhere are living longer, and the proportion of old people
in the community tends continually to increase. The
longer people live, the greater are the chances that they
will tend to become "castaways" in society. The church
especially, animated by a desire to minister in the name
of Christ to all persons, must discover ways to meet the
special spiritual needs of these older members. It has
been found in experience that older people frequently
enjoy group activity, since so many of their hours are
spent in lonely preoccupation with themselves and their
own memories. The church, which is essentially a group-
centered body, out of its wisdom in corporate experience,
should be able to deal adequately with this need to relate
the older members to others in an atmosphere of creative
fellowship.

There are also other groups with which the church
must keep in contact in a dynamic way: those who are in

hospitals or who are chronically ill; the feebleminded of all ages; the mentally sick; those who live in isolated places, as well as those who are passed by unnoticed in the great urban centers. In the church we are to be to one another as Christ is to each of us. This golden insight is the touchstone of Christian work with persons of every age and condition.

When we come down to the actual teaching work of the church, in classes and groups, we shall find that some method of grading according to age or capacity is desirable. In many countries, curriculum materials have been produced to assist in this task. The teachers who deal with pupils week by week or day by day will find that they are helped in their efforts to communicate the gospel by using materials and ideas suited to the mental age and social experience of their students. Those who prepare such materials are educators who have spent much time in relating subject matter to the needs and capacities of age groups with which they are professionally familiar.

The church will be stronger in its total life when every person feels that he is a truly participating member in the life of the total fellowship. Separate activities for age groups could conceivably become ends in themselves, if the total parish life were fragmented and divisive. But when the central worshiping community draws all together, the life of worship itself is enriched because of the joy and achievement that each age has been able to experience in the smaller fellowships grouped according to age and need.

4:

Through
Many
Channels

THE CHURCH *has* to teach, both because of the need to make sure that the gospel is handed on from generation to generation in the world and because of the sharing impulse which lies at the root of the fellowship of Christians in the church.

Once having recognized this need to teach, the church has to face the practical question as to how it shall proceed with its teaching task. One part of the church's task, a more theoretical part, is the effort to understand the faith in all its details, and to bring together all the details into a system of theology. In contrast to this, the task of the church in religious education belongs to what is usually called "practical theology." It is so regarded at least in the theological seminaries where young men and women are trained for professional vocational service in the church.

There is no essential conflict between systematic theology or historical theology and those aspects of theology called "practical" or "pastoral." When systematic theology views itself as an end, the result often is a kind of dryness and aridity. Theology as an intellectual pursuit, in and of itself, can become a lifeless undertaking. A live theology is always deeply related at all points to the actual life of the church as it pursues its God-given destiny and work in the midst of people in the situations where they have to live and work. Thus it is always desirable for those who like to construct theological systems, or those who like to talk about theology, to test their thinking at every point along the line by the rigorous demands of a church that has a divinely appointed work to do in the world. This is the warning we sounded earlier when we referred to the danger of indulging in propositions—looking at theological doctrines from the outside, as it were, without participating in the realities to which the doctrines refer. On the other hand, the so-called practical theological disciplines can become so much busywork, a bundle of techniques having little connection with the divine mission of the church, unless the practical work of the church is related to the underlying purpose, which it is the task of theology to study and to understand. For this reason those who are being prepared for professional leadership as pastors, deacons, deaconesses, youth workers, teachers, evangelists, and missionaries, should have an opportunity to be exposed at the same time to both the more theoretical and the more practical concerns. When we talk about God's redemption of the world through Jesus Christ, we ought to seek for ways in which this great redemption can be made known to mankind effectively and winningly.

When the affirmation is made that the Holy Spirit operates in the community of Christians to provide divine guidance, we need also to examine the life of the church and the various human means by which it is carried on, to ascertain whether we are blocking or assisting the work of the Holy Spirit. When we speak of the sacrament of Holy Communion as a sign and seal of our salvation, we need also to examine the manner in which the grace of this sacrament can extend into our common life.

The distinction between "systematic" and "practical" theology is of special concern to professional church workers; but we mention this matter here because every thoughtful layman and laywoman needs, though in a less technical way, to understand this relationship between Christian theory and Christian practice. For it is on the practical parish level that the faith expresses itself in the day-by-day existence of people. The full-time Christian worker is set apart in a special way to minister. But every Christian is a minister, in the sense that he is a living vessel, and all of us are called to be workmen who need not to be ashamed. It is our privilege to study constantly, in order that all aspects of our common life may reflect the imprint of our Lord. If we wish to be Christ's followers, we must recognize that nothing less than this is required of us.

What are the ingredients, then, of practical theology as it affects all members of the church? Conduct of worship will be largely in the hands of the professional clergy, although lay people, too, should have occasion frequently to lead in worship. Many churches provide for lay readers, local preachers, licentiates (the various churches use different names for the same office), whose duty it is to conduct services in the absence of the clergy, or to take services in places which do not have the regular services of an ordained minister, or to assist the clergy. Furthermore, even though one may not be going to conduct worship regularly, full participation in the life of worship requires that one be familiar with the forms of service, the reasons for which certain actions are performed, and the materials used in the services. In addition to this, we can cite the ministry to persons in need—a role in which laymen can be immensely helpful—that is often called "counseling." The organization and functioning of the various parts of the church's corporate life belong here also, as do the various forms of Christian education.

Whenever Christians engage in some part of practical church work, they are, in a sense, being educated. For we learn through experience, and all the activities to which we give our interest and attention become means through which we learn something that we did not know before. But, with all this, it is necessary for the church to be consciously engaged in a teaching ministry. Not every congregation will be able to make use of all the possible methods; a selection has to be made of those methods which are best suited to the particular situation in which the congregation has to work and witness. Basically, organized Christian education means the use of time and facilities. After determining how much time is available or desirable for specific religious instruction, a congregation is faced with the necessity of examining the channels open to it and making a choice among them as to which are the proper ones to emphasize. A program should not become static, in the sense that one or two forms of education are adopted and remain the only ones ever to be used. Changing circumstances will sometimes indicate the wisdom of abandoning one approach, or modifying it, and putting more accent on some other channel.

We shall now proceed to look briefly at some of the channels open to congregations. Some of these will be more suitable to one situation than to another, but this bird's-eye view of the manifold opportunities available to churches for their choosing should indicate something of the broader scope which is always possible for this phase of the church's life.

1. *Religious Instruction in the State Schools.* Where this is legally possible, churches certainly will want to take advantage of the time offered for this purpose. The energy of the church might well be poured into the training of teachers in religious knowledge (as in normal schools or training colleges), so that those who do this teaching might be thoroughly qualified both in knowledge of the subject and in the best activities for teaching it. Teachers do communicate their understanding of religion by what they themselves are, even in cases where they do not verbally indoctrinate persons in religion.

2. *Religious Instruction in Time Released from the State Schools.* In some countries the laws prohibit the teaching of religion in any form in the schools themselves, but the educational authorities are permitted to release children a certain number of hours each month to go to their churches for classes during the school day.

This pattern has been developed extensively in the United States of America. The churches themselves, usually working on a cooperative basis in a single community, are required to provide suitable textbooks, teachers, and classrooms. Usually the school boards require that the standards of instruction be equivalent to those maintained in the local state schools.

3. *Church Day Schools.* Where finances permit and the law allows, some churches operate complete day schools. These are operated independently as private schools. This is possible also in some countries where the state schools provide instruction in what is the established religion of the state but where some parents belonging to a religious community other than that supported by the state desire to have their children brought up under the influence of the family's own communion or persuasion. Since such schools are private schools, the churches sponsoring them are completely free to plan the curriculum in every part, to inculcate denominational loyalty, and to include worship as an integral part of the school day. These schools are always expensive to operate. Sometimes there is a tendency for their general quality to be inferior to that of the state schools, since the churches find it so difficult to raise the money necessary for the maintenance of a well-qualified staff and a high standard of equipment. The parochial school is the fundamental unit of instruction in the Roman Catholic educational system. A few Protestant denominations have adopted the same policy, although most American Protestants disapprove of parochial schools. Many missions have opened schools of a private kind, open to

Christians and non-Christians alike. In some countries such schools, while retaining complete freedom of religious instruction, have received large grants of money from the state in support of their work. This has been especially true in countries of the British Commonwealth.

4. *Religious Instruction After School Hours.* The Eastern Orthodox Church and the Jewish communities in some countries have for many years successfully operated classes for school children after the regular daily school hours, either every day of the week or on several week days. This has been designed to give the students detailed instruction in the faith and practice of their own religious group, such as could not be communicated to the children in general school classes. The same pattern has been adopted with varying approaches by other religious bodies. Sometimes special after-school classes are held during Advent and Lent, if not regularly.

5. *Vacation Church Schools.* During the summer or winter vacation periods, or at any other season that the children are not in school, they usually have a considerable amount of free time. Churches can capture a certain amount of this time each day, five days a week, in addition to the Sunday church school, thus providing a period of uninterrupted and continuous instruction in religion. These schools often are very appealing to children, for they provide a useful and interesting way in which to make use of spare time in the holidays. Courses of study can be used which cover in a concentrated way material that otherwise might have to be spread over a much longer time.

6. *Summer Conferences and Camps.* Formerly designed primarily for children and young people of twelve to seventeen years of age, these conferences or camps are now held for younger or older groups as well. They are held at some central place, preferably at some retreat or conference center, at which it is possible to accommodate a considerable number of children. However, sometimes the enrollment is deliberately limited to smaller numbers. Teachers are often supplemented with "counselors," who are usually adults who live with the children in bungalows or tents. These counselors seek to get to know the children individually and to deal personally with religious questions as these come up naturally in private and group conversations. Frequently an emphasis is placed on informal activities in addition to short courses of study. Such activities include outdoor hymn singing around campfires, worship services at rustic altars, hikes through the woods, and recreation such as swimming, boating, and games. Sometimes such conferences are organized by churches or fellowships of churches belonging to one denomination; but sometimes they have been planned to bring together children of several denominations. Conferences may be held for young people in general or for such special groups as the leaders or officers of youth groups in a certain area.

7. *Family Camps.* A development of recent years is the church family camp. The purpose of this is to bring together a number of families for a weekend or longer at a place where they can enjoy intensive fellowship together. Some activities are engaged in by the families as a whole, such as meals, worship, and games. Some of the

time is spent by the members divided up into suitable groups. Adequate quiet times and rest periods are planned in an ordered day. Those who have participated in such family camps feel that these camps provide a unique opportunity for young families to meet together as fellow Christians in an atmosphere of simple friendship; they help each family to deepen and strengthen its loyalty to the life of the church. Here families can discuss together their common problems and needs and can create the atmosphere of Christian fellowship in which an answer to these problems can and should be sought.

8. *Youth Clubs.* These are either for boys and girls together or separately. Usually meetings are times for study and friendship activities closely interrelated. Sometimes the clubs are sponsored by one adviser or by a married couple. In some cases the time of the meetings is on Sunday evening; in other cases the meeting is held on a weekday, either at the church or in someone's home. Often the meeting begins with a common meal.

9. *Organized Classes and Clubs Sponsored by the Young Men's Christian Association or the Young Women's Christian Association.* These organizations, international in scope, have served the youth of many lands for over a century. In some countries more than in others, they are the agencies to which the church looks for leadership in Christian youth work. Originally designed to provide Christian fellowship for young working men and women who often were not active in churches, they have enlarged their services to include many kinds of activities for children, youth, and adults. In some cities the YMCA and YWCA have established buildings

that serve as recreational centers for youth, these facilities being made available to the churches to supplement their own direct work with young people.

10. *Men's and Women's Organizations.* Meetings bring adults together for inspirational addresses and discussions. Service projects of a wide variety are undertaken. Funds are raised to support the church's ministries. Young married couples' groups, or organizations for older men and women, have been appearing in increasing numbers as the newest form of adult organization in the church. Groups organized on an interest basis are also appearing, such as those for social action projects or religious drama.

11. *Student Groups.* University and college students have been a vital factor in the national life of many countries. University students' gatherings to protest against some policy or to advocate some reform have been notable in Europe and Asia. In Great Britain and the United States of America much thought has been devoted by religious leaders, particularly chaplains, seminary professors, and administrators, to what is often called "the university problem." In many universities throughout the world today the atmosphere is thoroughly secular, in contrast to the earlier periods of the universities when religion was often at the very heart of the life of teachers and students. How can the Christian faith be reinterpreted to the present student generation so that there can be a renewal of concern with religion on the part of faculty and students alike? There are now many student religious societies that have been organized by one church or another; others, like the Stu-

dent Christian Movement, bring together students of many different bodies. These groups often provide a link with the religious life for students who in the academic environment of the university find themselves cut off from the religious traditions to which they have been accustomed. There seems to be unlimited scope for the extension of such work as this in the newer nations of Asia and Africa.

12. *The Sunday Church School*. In 1780 Robert Raikes of Gloucester, England, a printer and philanthropist, gathered some boys on Sunday, their one day free from work in the mills, into a small school which he had set up, with the aim of providing these children with some rudiments of learning. Most of them had not had an opportunity to learn to read or write. Most of the time in these first Sunday schools was spent in what might be regarded as secular studies, but time was found for a certain amount of teaching in religion as well. The idea of having a school on Sunday took root and developed rapidly. It soon outgrew its original context, since weekday schools rapidly took over the work of general education. Sunday schools were now occupied principally with religious instruction, some of them running with both morning and afternoon sessions. At first some church leaders were doubtful of the plan, but eventually the church adopted the Sunday school as a basic medium for religious education. The result was the flowering of the great movement of modern Christian education. Several things were characteristic of the Sunday school movement. It was largely a lay movement at its inception. It was frequently interdenominational, until the

denominations accepted the pattern of the Sunday
school for their individual use. It was concerned not only
with children but with adults as well, adult classes becoming a standard part of the approach. The Sunday
school movement took on an international character
when the World Sunday School Association was established (in 1906, under the name The International Sunday School Association). The worldwide conventions of
that organization and its successor, the World Council
of Christian Education and Sunday School Association,
have continued across many years to attract leaders and
workers from every country where Sunday schools exist.

The Sunday school movement was at first quite hap-
hazard. The first great step forward was in the provision
of plans and materials for teaching—first on a uniform
basis, the same lesson for all ages each Sunday; then on
a graded basis, lessons designed for use with the different
age groups. At present practically every church publishes
an "official" curriculum for religious education and
sponsors staffs of specialists who are available to give
counsel to the churches.

Because the term "Sunday school" seemed to connote
primarily an activity referring to Sunday only, there has
been a tendency in recent times to use the designation
"Sunday church school." This connotes the school of the
whole church in the form of that part of the school meeting on Sundays. Weekday church school, vacation church
school, and other terms refer to the school of the church
meeting at the other times indicated.

Whereas in the beginning of the Sunday schools, religious education often was handled as a work almost inde-

pendent of the churches, though related to them, now the educational work of the church has been more fully integrated into the whole life and program of the church. This is reflected in the provision of more adequate financial support for educational work in local parishes, in the appointment or election of Christian education committees and superintendents by the whole parish, and in some large churches by the choice of one single head for the whole of this work, a person who has full professional status and is known as the Director of Christian Education.

13. *The Confirmation Class.* Preparation for admission to full membership or adult communicant status has been traditionally accomplished by means of confirmation or church membership classes. These are sometimes open to all inquirers, those being confirmed and adults being received into membership after completing the course of study. Such courses range from a few weeks to several years in length. Sometimes adults are taught separately from older children and young people. Normally the confirmation class is taught by the chief pastor of the congregation, whose solemn responsibility and privilege it is to assist those who plan to make a renewal of their baptismal vows or a public profession of their faith in the presence of God and the congregation. The clergyman who fulfills this task is sharing preeminently in a teaching ministry, as distinguished from the preaching or sacramental function of his ministry.

14. *Fellowship Groups for Witnessing and Study.* Living in a secular world as well as in the Christian community, Christians have found it helpful to form in a

congregation small groups of persons who will consider
together ways of witnessing to their faith. Sometimes
these groups are organized on the basis of a common
occupation; for example, in Germany workers in indus-
trial plants sometimes meet in small groups to pray,
study the Bible, and address themselves to the question
of how they can best witness to their faith while at work.
There is also a real value in forming groups whose membership cuts across social or vocational lines. Both the
young adult and the older person find it possible to share
deeply in such a spiritual "cell group," each strengthening
the other. In the small group it is possible for people to
learn to be utterly candid with one another, for pre-
tenses fade away as people experience together the personal power of a comon faith. In such circles it is possible to face questions like these: How can we bear witness to our faith to those who are quite untouched by
Christ, without forcing ourselves on others? How shall
we as Christians meet in freedom with our Jewish neighbors, witnessing to them concerning our faith without at
the same time seeming to show discourtesy or disrespect
to them and to their tradition, in which we, too, share?
How much of our heritage of faith is reserved for those
committed to Christ, and how much can be shared with
those who are not yet called into the church? Answers
to questions such as these are not easily arrived at, but
in small groups meeting for prayer and study, when "two
or three" gather in the Lord's name and presence, the
Holy Spirit can be trusted to shed light and to impart
needed wisdom.

5: Through Many Methods

MANY OLDER PEOPLE who were brought up as children in Sunday schools share a certain picture of that experience which is remarkably uniform in many lands and in many types of churches. The traditional Sunday school class consisted of what has sometimes been called facetiously the "huddle method." Small groups of children would sit around a teacher in a large room, where many similar classes were being held at the same time. The class sessions would be preceded by a general opening act of worship for the entire school, and followed by similar closing exercises.

Frequently, under such circumstances, the teacher was confined to the simplest methods of teaching. Sometimes the pupils would read one by one from the Bible or from a quarterly magazine containing a set of lessons. The teacher would ask questions, which would be answered in turn by the children, sometimes after they had refreshed their memory by looking up the passage which had just been read. The noise from surrounding classes, although kept down through disciplinary restraint to a hushed hubbub, nevertheless constituted a real barrier to earnest concentration. The only possible method of teaching was to keep the children seated throughout, and any method that involved action or movement was out of the question. As often as not, especially in very small churches that did not have a Sunday school hall or parish rooms, the class would even be occupying pews in the main church, the teacher standing facing the pupils, with his back to the altar or pulpit.

Such circumstances still prevail in many places. In more developed congregations, however, Sunday church school teaching has come a long way from that early period. Many smaller churches suffer very much from the limitation of space; and sometimes large congregations have preferred to continue the "huddle method" out of force of habit or because this was thought to be a good method of teaching, or because of space considerations. By and large, the churches have realized that we shall get better teaching in the church only if we pay attention to securing the best methods of teaching. Secular education has advanced in the matter of method far beyond the old-fashioned "spare the rod and spoil the child" psychology. During the last fifty years, experimental psychology has made great progress and among other things has devoted a great deal of attention to the processes of learning and teaching. These scientific discoveries about the nature of the learning process have been widely published, although no one would say that the last word has yet been said. The results have been influential in changing the methods of teaching in practically every subject, in languages and mathematics as well as literature, writing, and history. It is to be expected that the teaching of religion should also be affected by a better understanding of the learning process. A whole book would be needed if we were to go into detail about these changes. Perhaps all that is needed here is to point out certain specially important features in them.

For one thing, it has been found that persons, children as well as adults, learn through doing. This is a very old truth which was not unknown to the ancient Greeks. But the modern form of this principle has expressed itself in a mode of teaching that takes into consideration various ways of approaching any desired subject matter. It is no longer supposed just because children have learned a certain number of words that they will equally well understand what those words mean. This is as true of religious learning as it is of any other kind of learning. Children may be able to repeat from memory, through drill over a long period of time, many biblical passages which they would be at a loss to explain in their own words. This is because they have learned words but lack the understanding of the meaning of those words. The modern religious teacher may still want pupils to memorize passages of scripture, yet the approach will be different. If a modern teacher wants a class to learn a particular passage, how does he set about it? Drill is used only sparingly. The passage is examined from many directions and in many ways. The class talks about the passage; perhaps expressing it in visual form through drawing or projected slides, acting it out in dramatic form, or writing about it in notebooks or in creative stories and poems reflecting an understanding of the passage. Even this is not a full account of the methods that can be used. Not every approach is used in every instance; the teacher chooses the methods that seem best suited to the class and its growing understanding.

If we are going to have new methods, we shall probably have to discover a new setting in which these methods can be effective. The separate classroom for each class may be a luxury which relatively few congregations or parishes can afford. Whatever the situation, a rethinking of the way in which we allot our available space can often produce more satisfactory results. Even a one-room church can sometimes produce a setting for more imaginative teaching than is possible merely by having the classes sit in the pews. They might well remain there for quieter portions of their lesson. But they could use the outdoors, if the weather is warm, for some part of the class session. Possibly a nearby house or hall could be "borrowed" for some classes to use. It is also possible to stagger the sessions, some classes meeting earlier and others later, so that not all the classes will be meeting at the same time.

Another principle that is now quite generally accepted is that of grading the pupils according to age and intelligence. In general, there are two grading systems used: (1) *Closely graded*, which means having a class for each age corresponding to the public school classes; that is, separate classes for ages three, four, five, six, seven, eight, and so on. The adult classes are not graded in the same manner, of course, but are divided into young adult and older adult classes, or perhaps according to interests. This plan is suitable only for quite large Sunday church schools. (2) *Group-graded*, which means that for teaching purposes the children will be put into manageable groups on a broader scale, where division exactly according to age is not possible. Children who are still too young to be at school will form one of these groups. Children in the first two or three grades of the public school might be another group, and so on. The groupings may be arranged in a wide variety of ways, usually reflecting the groupings in the local school system. For example, one group would probably be all those in the upper grades of high school, if these children are enrolled together in similar classes in the public school.

The reason for grading classes is so that teaching can be molded according to the pupils' capacity to learn. The psychological differences of children at the various age levels can be kept in mind as the teaching materials are prepared and the lesson plans made by the teacher. Also, children respond more completely to class situations that are designed for their particular interests and capacities and that result in their becoming personally interested and involved in what is being done. The teachers' task is made easier by allowing teachers to become really skilled workers with one age group. This means they do not have to spread themselves over too wide an age range. This means also that teachers can be assigned to work with children of an age which they find most congenial. Not every teacher can be expected to be equally adept at teaching three-year-olds and eleven-year-olds.

Children are different from one another and grow up at different speeds. This means that at any age there are certain things that a child is likely to be able to learn and other things that he is unlikely to be able to learn. Observers over a wide area agree that the lessons each child is able to learn, as well as the experiences that he is able to make his own, depend largely on his own individual rate of inner growth. If we take children of about the same age, we shall certainly find that in many ways they are like one another. For example, most children would seem to be ready to learn how to read at the age of five or six. But, though in most respects children of the same age may be like one another, it still remains a fact that each individual is himself and no one else. If some pupils show more alacrity in certain types of learning than others at a given time, the reason is to be looked for in a certain readiness or lack of readiness in the personality. The teacher can encourage a child to develop an interest in a particular phase of learning, surrounding him with incentives and encouragement; but no teacher will be able to coerce a child into doing that for which the growth of his body and the development of his mind have not yet prepared him.

This has relevance for Christian education in two ways. First, this explanation makes it clear why some children show more eagerness than others for religious studies and experience. Some children will be greatly interested in uniting with the church at the age of nine, while many will be quite unready for this step until they are fourteen or older. Custom or policy might provide a reason for arranging for all children to be confirmed or admitted to membership of the church at a certain definite age; but we must not assume just because they all happen to be of the same age that they will all be equally ready in mind and spirit. Second, teachers dealing with puipls in a class should be more patient and more careful to get to know each individual child if they are aware that not all children can grow in religious understanding at the same speed and that not all will be ready to undertake the same tasks at the same time. Although teaching with an eye on individuals as well as on the group as a whole may make much heavier demands on the teacher, the ultimate results will be more satisfying. The aim of the teacher will be to provide opportunities for each individual child to grow in the faith according to his own capacity to respond to the various levels of reality that are revealed to us in the gospel.

Psychologists have produced considerable data within the last two decades concerning the developmental tasks of children as well as of older people. We know that young children have a need to become aware of themselves as separate from their surroundings and from their parents. This need is accompanied by a craving for affection and the beginning of an adjustment to others' expectations. In later childhood the task is to free themselves from identification with adults in their world, so that they can become persons in their own right. This becomes accentuated in adolescence, at which age children are beginning to enter into their own adulthood. This is symbolized by the various rites of initiation which the adult society has set up to recognize the adolescent's arrival at the age of full responsibility. Yet the complete awareness of selfhood and its accompanying responsibility does not arrive until one takes his place as an independent wage earner, homemaker, and member of the community. This is merely a suggestion of the type of understanding of growing selfhood that modern psychologists have set forth. The important insight as far as Christian education is concerned lies in the recognition of the inner dynamics of personal development, for religious experience is not separate from, but is deeply tied in with, the total development of a personality at every stage of life.

In recent years, more attention has been paid than in earlier times to the nature of group experience. People always have lived and worked in groups. The Christian community has laid the greatest stress on group life, because of the corporate nature of the Body of Christ itself. It might have been expected that the experiences of Christians living and working together in the church would have made any new emphasis on group experience quite superfluous. However, it has been taken far too much for granted that the church is really experiencing the fullness of the life of what a Christian group ought to be. Yet the fellowship falls far short of what it ought to be if the church were living up to the ideal of its life as that is shown to us in the gospel.

This can be seen sometimes in congregations where certain "natural" leaders take over much of the responsibility for leadership year after year. The congregation needs to understand that leadership itself is something for which people can be trained and that the only way in which they can be trained for it is by being given responsible tasks to do. Or again, in some Sunday church school classes, the teacher unconsciously has let himself be the center of the class' approaches to almost everything that comes up. He makes all the plans for everything that is going to be done throughout the whole program. He personally desires to *tell* the children what he thinks they should know.

The newer emphases put a great deal of effort into making each group situation an experience in which all truly share. This does not mean that the teacher or leader gives up his position of leadership. Rather he reinterprets his role, thinking of himself as a guide rather than as a director. He never compels; he persuades vigorously, but without going so far as to turn persuasion into compulsion. He does not make all the plans personally, but knows how to delegate responsibility, always taking the members of the group into his confidence, as together they talk over the plans for all that they are going to do. They jointly arrive at desirable and desired goals and share the executing of the work that needs to be done in connection with tasks agreed upon. The value of such an approach is that it develops leadership according to capacity and makes everyone in the group feel that he is a participant in a mutually worthwhile and even thrilling enterprise. Sometimes this method may seem to be less efficient, since it means allotting more time for discussions of procedure. Decisions cannot be reached nearly as quickly as when one person takes responsibility for making all of them. However, the leader who learns to deal with groups in this manner discovers the joy of really belonging to a group and identifying himself with it wholeheartedly.

Space will permit the mention of only one other trend: the influence on teaching methods of the new psychological discoveries and of the knowledge that they have given us of the deeper levels of the mind. We know now that the mind is not separate from the body, and that furthermore the mind itself is most complex in its make-up. Subconscious and even unconscious factors exist in our minds and continually affect the way our minds work. Thus, when we face our pupils, we are not merely writing on blank tablets. Nor is the teacher himself merely the result of actions that have come upon him from outside. Everyone who comes to us comes with his own peculiar combination of personal factors. This is as true of the teacher coming to meet his pupils as it is for persons in other situations. The religious appeal must be made not only to the rational mind but to our pupils' real selves, their complete personalities. The findings of the newer psychologies tend to be in keeping with the Christian understanding of man as he is depicted in the Bible. As the apostle Paul well knew, we are not simply clay to be molded in the manner that the teacher or leader might desire. We are *persons*—in whom the depth of evil exists as well as the aspiration after goodness. We are capable of having conflicts raging inside us even while outwardly all may appear placid and serene. We can invent excuses to cover up our mistakes and our sins. We do what we ought not to do, and we leave undone the things we should do.

Not every teacher can be expected to be a trained

psychologist. It is dangerous to assume that we ought even to pretend to have any great understanding of the complexity of human nature and conduct. In this, as in most other aspects of life, "a little learning is a dangerous thing." But one simple thing which every teacher can do is to remember that the church is not simply a company of saints; it is also a community of sinners. This is why we all need to confess our sins to God. If only the teacher will remember this, it will guard him against being overoptimistic about what can be accomplished in the class through giving to the pupils sound moral instruction and good advice. It will also protect the teacher from the delusion that he can make saints. Only God can do that. The teacher's function is to accept the persons who come to him as they are, with all their foibles, weaknesses, and shortcomings. In so doing he should recognize that he too, in his own way, is a man, subject to all the same imperfections. However, the good teacher will ever strive to relate his methods to the pupils in such a manner that the faith can speak relevantly to each of them in his actual condition, and to all of them together in their common situation.

Let us now look briefly at several methods, each of which can be used effectively with most groups at one time or another.

1. *Conversation.* This seems almost too obvious to mention; yet because it is obvious, teachers often fail to notice what immense possibilities it has as a teaching method. Conversation is human relationship through words. In the class situation both teacher and pupils take part in this kind of relationship. The questions should

not all emanate from the teacher, nor all the answers. Nor should a lesson plan be so rigidly constructed that a teacher is afraid to follow a fresh angle for as long a time as it seems to be profitable for the group. Sometimes conversation may seem to be a mere waste of time; yet in the end it may be found to have led the pupils to deep insights that they could hardly have reached in any other way.

2. *Discussion.* Discussion differs from simple conversation only in the sense that it is more definitely directed to a specific question or area of subject matter and more consciously organized. The key to effective discussion is that once the question under consideration is set forth, either by the teacher or by a pupil appointed in advance to be the discussion leader, all in the group be given an opportunity to contribute by the expression of their ideas. Discussion can be carried on in various ways. One method is to arrange for the presentation of a different aspect of the question by a number of speakers; then group discussion follows upon the various points that have been raised. In a debate, two opposing sides of a question are set forth by selected speakers who assemble their arguments in a formal way. This is followed by an opportunity for the audience to introduce ideas or questions. In an "open-ended" story, the teacher or leader tells a story up to a point, which leaves open a number of different possibilities as to the way in which the story might end. The narrative goes only to the point at which the alternatives must be faced. The discussion then takes the form of examining these possible solutions and perhaps choosing among them. In another discussion form,

the class or group is broken down into smaller groups of only a few persons, each group being invited to discuss a subject presented by the leader. Each small group has a recorder, who then reports back to the whole group. This technique makes it possible to include everyone in an intimate give-and-take as well as in the discussion carried on by the whole group.

3. *Constructive and Creative Activities.* A contructive activity consists of making something. Thus a class might construct a Palestinian village of the type with which Jesus was familiar. A creative activity, on the other hand, involves expressing a reaction to something that has been studied. For example, after studying a passage of the Bible together, the teacher might ask the pupils to draw a picture expressing their understanding of the incident. The same thing might be done in the form of writing a story or a poem.

4. *Audio-visual Methods.* Slides, filmstrips, motion pictures, flat pictures, flannelgraphs and other forms of audio-visual aids are now available in most countries for church use. These usually require a certain amount of equipment—especially in the case of projected pictures— some of which is costly. Also, teachers must be instructed in how to use these instruments; or else someone must be found who knows how to use them and is willing to give his services to the church in this way. Audio-visual aids can be vitally helpful as aids to teaching. They must not, however, be regarded either as means to fill in otherwise unused time, or as ends in themselves; they are to be used either as means of imparting information rapidly or as means of promoting discussion in the groups.

5. *Storytelling.* The narrative form has always occupied an important place in religious teaching. This is to be seen in the use made of it in the Bible. The story conveys a truth, not as a set of propositions but in the form of a series of situations drawn from life; the listener has the opportunity of entering by imagination into those situations and identifying himself with the various characters in turn. Stories that are most effective in religious teaching are those that are simple but penetrating. The art of telling stories is not easily mastered by all, but it is worth every teacher's effort to become reasonably adept at it.

6. *Dramatization.* Another form of teaching that has many possibilities is the acting out of stories. Here too, as in storytelling, the value lies in identification with the characters. Both those who enact the dramatic situation and those who watch it are involved in the action or the dilemma or the situation. Biblical stories lend themselves very well to informal dramatization. In the informal type, the action and words are improvised with very little advance preparation, following a class' study of the Bible or other material. Sometimes a written script is used, especially when it is desired to share the dramatization with another class or with visitors, as on a parents' visiting day.

7. *Role Playing.* This also is a form of storytelling, a variety of dramatization. It is more spontaneous than even informal dramatization. A problem situation is presented by the teacher, who then assigns persons to act out a simple sequence. Members of the group are asked to identify with the reactions to the problem made by the

characters being depicted. When the role playing is ended, the group proceeds to analyze why the various characters acted as they did and to make a critique on the basis of some Christian insight.

8. *Resource People.* Often a class' consideration of some question can be enriched and clarified by asking someone to visit the class to make a contribution from his own special knowledge of the subject. This person might be asked to give a brief talk, or to be prepared to answer questions. This, incidentally, is a very good way in which to involve adult members of the church in the educational program. Some people who have no special ability for teaching might nevertheless be quite willing to share their skills or knowledge with the group. For example, a science teacher might be brought in when the class is studying the creation of the world, to help the students to see the differences between the religious and scientific approaches to the study of nature and life. A person who knows how to make various constructive items, such as puppets, could come in for one or more sessions to help the teacher and pupils become skillful in the use of a certain method.

This is only a short list of teaching methods available to the Sunday or weekday religious teacher, to the pastor in his confirmation class, or to the leader of a youth group. Many other possible methods such as field trips, exhibits, and interviews could be added to the list. All who teach religion should be encouraged to use imagination and to adjust their methods to the situation in which they have to teach. Any method is only a means to the larger end of communicating the Christian gospel.

6: By
Devoted
Teachers

THE ESSENCE of the Christian religion is not the transmission of information so much as the communication of a quality of life, the New Being in Christ. It follows, therefore, that those responsible for the teaching task of the church will fulfill their vocation only if they are truly committed disciples of their Lord, carrying out in practice the requirements of the faith they profess.

A glorious aspect of the Sunday school movement in its first decades was that it was almost entirely a lay movement. Sometimes members of the clergy were hesitant to take up the Sunday school as an agency of the church's work, because they feared it would supplant the church itself in people's loyalty. That fear was justified in some instances, in places where Sunday school was not integrated with other parts of the local church but had a kind of independent and separate existence of its own. Yet the early fears were soon succeeded by a genuine enthusiasm on the part of ministers, once they saw that the Sunday school could become a valuable help in the total life of the Christian church.

Throughout the years, hundreds of thousands of devoted men and women have responded to invitations to become teachers in the church. In many cases, young people discovered through serving as volunteer teachers in the Sunday school that they had a calling to Christian service in the pastoral ministry, in overseas missionary work, or in professional religious education. The Sunday church school thus became and continues to be a major recruiting ground for those who later prepare for professional church work as well as a training ground for consecrated lay leadership.

In recent years the meaning of Christian vocation has been presented by theologians and preachers in new ways and with a number of new insights. The older view that the "call" of God was especially applicable to the ordained clergy is being replaced or enriched by the view that every man, woman, and child is called by God to certain functions and tasks, each according to the talents, capabilities, and insights with which he or she is endowed. This is essentially the recovery of the biblical view of vocation. Each person is given a life by God, and it is in response to him that each is required to make his decisions as to how he will use his time, energy, and money. The "call" applies not only to the type of daily work in which one is engaged, but also to the use of one's leisure time. It is exactly at this point that some will be called to use their free time for various aspects of the church's life and ministry. Some will do parish visitation; others will feel that they can serve best by singing in the choir or by assisting in the life of another church group. And doubtless some among them will feel the special call to teach.

What are some of the qualifications that we ought to be able to expect in those who would teach in the church? We are thinking now of volunteer teachers in the Sunday church school, although the same qualifications would seem to have equal validity for those who are engaged in religious teaching on a full-time basis.

In the first place, a teacher of religion should be himself a person of faith. If he is to be the channel through whom the Holy Spirit can reach others, he must be in living relationship with God through Christ. This does not mean that one has to have attained the fullest height of religious experience; and it certainly does not mean that one will presume to suggest to others that he is a model Christian. Rather, he is to be thought of as one who lives by the grace of God, constantly turning to him as the source of all he is and has. He will know in his personal life the richness of redemption. The redeemed person finds himself entering a new relationship to others. He makes no effort to keep to himself what God has given him. The Christian life retains its luster and beauty only insofar as it is released into the lives of others.

This means, in the second place, that the teacher will be a witness. He will not so much share with others exactly pound for pound, as it were, what he has received. He will seek primarily to give expression to the great realities of faith, knowing that the Holy Spirit may choose to express himself differently in others' lives from what has been the expression in his own. That is, a good teacher will not so much want to have the pupils become like himself as to encourage them to become truly themselves, as God has created them; in terms of their own God-given personalities.

Furthermore, a good teacher will be a friend to his pupils. A real friend is as much a good listener as a talker. He is always available, to be turned to when needed and to be sought after when his help is desired. Both children and adults need to have understanding friends who can sustain them in situations of need. A teacher has the unique opportunity to be a friend whose presence is strengthening and whose counsel springs out of a deep awareness of the pupils' inner selves.

It is almost a truism, but it should be said again and again, that a Christian teacher teaches most by example. What he is speaks more loudly than what he says. If he is himself a man of prayer, the pupils will know that his words about prayer spring from a knowledge of prayer. If he is faithful in all church responsibilities, the pupils will come to understand without being directly told that the church really deserves their loyalty and support as well.

The Christian teacher will never be primarily a technician, but he will recognize that good teaching requires careful planning and the use of clearly understood methods. For this reason he will always be alert to discover the best methods to use for a particular lesson or unit of study. He will try to avoid getting into the rut of always doing the same things in the same way. He will seek to make each session of the class radiantly interesting, and he will try to make use of every possible means to get the students themselves personally involved in all that is being done. Sometimes the word creative has been used to refer to this kind of teaching, as over against the dullness and monotony that result when one method is followed all the time and that produce bored and inattentive students. *Creative* in this sense does not mean making something altogether new; it means stirring something already given into vital flame.

The teacher will want to relate all that is done in the class sessions to the whole life of the congregation and of the larger church in the world. This is a point at which printed curriculum materials, now available for teachers' and pupils' use, can in many cases be helpful. Those who write the courses of study almost always suggest possible avenues for exploring an idea or using an activity that will lead the pupils into expanding horizons of the Christian life. The possibilities for this kind of larger frame of reference are ever growing in our world, as the Christian churches are rediscovering one another through the ecumenical movement. Although we use different forms, speak various languages, and emphasize different aspects of the gospel, we are all part of the total purpose of God for his world. The teacher fails to discharge one of his major responsibilities if he tends through his teaching to encourage only local, provincial types of Christians. Loyalty to a local body is essential and important, but it is a universal gospel of salvation that the church must teach and preach, and every Christian must become aware of his membership in the whole church of Christ in the world.

The Christian teacher has a dual role to fulfill. He is a

member of the church, sharing in the common life of the whole body; and at the same time he is the mentor and guide of the smaller company that constitutes his immediate class. The best teacher will be growing in two directions at the same time: in loyalty to the whole life of the church of Christ and in mastery of methods and techniques that will make him a better teacher of the particular group for which he has major responsibility. The two tasks enrich and supplement each other. He will be a better teacher when he is growing in vital church experience; and he will be a better church member as he carries out with imagination and devotion his individual duties as the teacher of a class.

We have set a very high standard for Christian teachers. Do people come forward possessing all the qualities simply as a result of their natural gifts, or can they be produced? It is obvious that not everyone will feel a calling to teach. Those who do feel such a vocation are the ones who are likely to offer their services in this connection. Thus a selective process has already taken place. We would not offer to build a bridge over a river if we knew nothing about fundamental principles of structural engineering. Nor is anyone likely to offer to teach if he finds the task repugnant to him. However, just as a person is likely to be attracted into engineering because of certain natural inclinations and abilities or talents, so one is likely to be drawn into teaching through the same kind of internal process.

Yet the would-be bridge designer must prepare for his task by extensive study. He must know something of physics, of tensions in metal, of materials, of weights and balances. He must understand geographical factors, such as winds and tides, and something of the preparation of plans, not to mention the methods employed in actual construction. If the Christian teacher is going to pursue his vocation seriously, he will also have to do some preliminary preparation. He must seek to improve his knowledge of human personality, the ways in which people learn, and the functioning of groups. He must become increasingly familiar with the Bible, with the history of the church, with liturgy, worship, prayer, and meditation. He cannot escape the necessity for doing some earnest thinking and studying in theology proper. All these matters are grist for the teacher's mill. They are the tools of his trade. Of course, not all the preparation in the world would make some people into effective teachers, whereas some people with a minimum of training are by nature quite capable teachers. Nor does a person ever reach the point of being able to say, "Now I am a master teacher and I need no further training." Christian humility forbids the making of any such claim. If we consider the vast body of knowledge which no one can ever hope to master in one field, no teacher is likely ever to claim that he has reached the point at which he need go no further.

It is the duty of the church to set up mediums through which teachers who are about to begin their work can get necessary foundations and advanced teachers can continue to improve their skills and knowledge.

There are several time-tested methods of teacher training (often called "leadership training"):

1. *Leadership Training Schools.* Within a city or an

area, a denomination or council of churches can set up annual training schools or institutes offering the range of courses needed in the locality. If these schools can be carried on jointly by churches of several denominations working together, all the churches are enriched by learning from one another's experience. Usually the courses will be offered in both methods and content. All teachers need to know more about the Bible, for example, and the best way to study the Bible is to dig into the actual biblical writings with the aid of an instructor who is familiar with these writings. The methods courses will be directed toward teachers of specific age groups such as we find in the Sunday church school departments. Teachers working with kindergarten children need to explore methods for that age; those working with pre-adolescent classes will have a different set of problems; while those working with adolescents will be facing other situations and different challenges.

2. *Summer Conferences.* Often during the summer months (in some countries, the winter months) people have more time available for concentrated study. Many teachers are willing to devote their vacations, or a part of them, to attending a leadership training institute. Ideally, such a conference or institute is held at a place in which visiting teachers can stay in reasonable comfort and where there are convenient classrooms and libraries for the purpose of teaching and study. Sometimes colleges or schools are willing to make their facilities available for these sessions. The same kinds of courses are offered as in regional training schools, except that the classes meet daily and a corporate experience is made possible through

worship, common meals, recreation, and singing. This program can be carried through on a more intensive level than can the through-the-week sessions of a regional school. It is especially valuable if a laboratory school (or "demonstration" school) can be linked up with the adults' courses. In such a school, children from the neighborhood can be enrolled in what is actually a species of model vacation school. The teachers in training can participate as helpers and observers, while the actual teaching of the children is conducted by skilled and experienced teachers.

3. *Local Leadership Training Schools.* Within a local parish or congregation it is possible to do some teacher training all during the year. This can take the form of six- or eight-week sessions during which the pastor or some other qualified person meets with the teachers of a department. In the case of small congregations, he may meet with the entire teaching staff to consider content or methods. All the teachers in the group might be asked to read in advance the same book, and this would constitute the text for the course. The advantage of this kind of training is that it is always specific and concrete rather than merely abstract or theoretical. It deals with the teaching work of the church in terms of the local situation. This is also an effective way of helping those who are just beginning to teach, or who are about to start, to find their feet in an unfamiliar world. Many persons understandably hesitate to take on full charge of a class because of lack of experience or because of doubt concerning their ability to teach. Still, they have expressed a willingness to consider the possibility and to learn how

to teach by a period of testing. If they can do this in company with friends and neighbors in a local leadership training class, they will be helped to overcome their shyness and to enter the good fellowship of those who already are engaged in Christian teaching.

4. *Workers' Conferences.* All teachers in a local church should be encouraged to share in workers' conferences held at regular intervals. These are times in which specific problems can be faced together or new skills mastered. These should also be times for the establishment of an *esprit de corps* in the fellowship. Many congregations find that when the teachers share a meal together prior to their formal meeting, a splendid group feeling and a high morale are fostered.

Here are some examples of "themes" suitable for a fruitful series of workers' conferences in a parish:

» What shall we do about the problems of discipline?

» How can we teach children concerning the worldwide outreach of the church?

» How can we reach children in our community who are not attached to a church?

» What should we do about adult education in our parish?

» How can we make the most of audio-visual methods of teaching?

» How much memory work should be used in our courses?

» What should we do concerning education in the principles of Christian family living?

» What are the underlying principles of our church's educational work?

» How can we learn to understand children better?

5. *Church Libraries.* Christians are deeply concerned with literacy because the Christian faith is basically bound up with the Bible. The reading of the Bible is important to the reception and transmission of the gospel by individuals and the whole company of the church. Knowledge of the Bible is only the beginning; to those who can read, a vast range of Christian knowledge and experience lies open. For this reason it is necessary to encourage people in the church to read the best Christian literature. No congregation is too small to start a library. The collection of books will grow in number as the idea gets established that responsible members in the church will develop in themselves the habit of Christian reading. Books can be circulated so that more and more people will have the opportunity to familiarize themselves with the various aspects of the Christian faith. It is especially desirable to include books on the teaching work of the church. The educational work of the parish will be improved as more people are introduced to the joys of study.

6. *Experimental Methods.* Denominations and sometimes local churches are currently showing a great deal of imagination in developing new forms of leadership training influenced by various group dynamics methods and by the newer approaches to curriculum. Team teaching, for example, in which two or more teachers share in the guidance of a class, provides opportunities for more

experienced teachers to impart helpful suggestions to less experienced teachers, who constitute the learning part of the team. In a local congregation certain persons who become recognized as especially competent teachers are sometimes "loaned" to other churches for brief periods during which they actually take over the direction of a class in order to demonstrate good teaching methods. Leadership training institutes and workshops have been developed in several denominations which have had to face the necessity of retraining large numbers of teachers in the use of new curriculums. This has been true particularly in the Lutheran Church in America, the United Church of Christ, and the Protestant Episcopal Church.

7:   In
Every
Home

THE CHRISTIAN RELIGION was taught long before the modern forms of schools and the highly organized life of modern congregations developed. Looking back at earlier centuries, we sometimes grow wistfully nostalgic, thinking that maybe in a simpler society the faith was more truly taught. Be that as it may, and however much we may regret it, it is not possible for us to go back to the past. Each age must develop its own formal plans and methods for education. The school was developed by the church as a response to a need. Originally this was the need to train a literate clergy; later, especially after the Reformation, it was the need of training a literate generation of practicing Christians to exercise their personal access to the Bible and to participate fully in the devotional life of the church. We have to face the problems of our own day, and we must try to find adequate answers to the questions that are posed by the circumstances of the day.

Even prior to the development of schools, however, the faith was taught, albeit in a much more informal way than that which is practiced in the schools. It was the home which had to bear the chief burden of instruction. In the bosom of the Christian family the young child was introduced to the realities of the spiritual life: prayer, Christian standards of conduct, and a consciousness of the religious meaning of birth, puberty, marriage, sin and forgiveness, and death. In the home were cultivated the pious practices encouraged by the church in successive generations. People learned a basic attitude toward life. The whole of their life was set in a Christian direction, even though they may not have had access to many books, or even to the Bible, the greatest book of all.

As suggested earlier, we learn through doing. Religious learning is no exception to this principle. A home passes on to the children the real attitudes and convictions of the parents with regard to religion, whether these are attitudes of consecrated Christian living, agnosticism, or even outright hostility. Hostility to religion is a kind of religious attitude in reverse. If a whole family goes regularly to worship services together, habits are formed that may be expected to stay with the children throughout their lives. If the clergy is criticized adversely or if other church members are condemned by the parents, or if life is viewed in superstitious terms, members of the younger generation will pick up such attitudes, almost without knowing that they are doing so. This has always been the case, and there is no reason to believe that the pattern today is essentially different.

Among the Jews, century after century, the prepara-

tions for the Passover feast in the homes of the faithful
have been carried out in such a manner as to elicit from
the children the question: "Why is this night different
from other nights?" Whereupon the father proceeds, as
he is enjoined to do by the Scriptures, to explain to the
children the great event of the exodus, which always has
been regarded by the Jews as the evidence of God's favor
toward his people in the covenant.

Christians did not carry on the distinctively Jewish
religious ceremonies such as the lighting of the Sabbath
candles, a weekly reminder of the foundation of the family's religious faith. Nevertheless, the Christian church
has never lost sight of the truth that the people who first
take a hand in the education of the young, and perhaps
exercise the strongest influence of all, are the parents.
Whether or not there was a conscious effort to inculcate
certain religious practices, the devout Christian parents
knew that they were accountable to God for introducing
their children by example and precept to the heritage of
faith.

This awareness characterizes the serious Christian
parents of today as well. The modern situation, however,
is infinitely more complex in practically every country
than it was even as recently as fifty years ago. In many
places parental authority is no longer taken as seriously
as it was once. The development of new mediums of
communication such as radio and television has brought
family life more definitely and relentlessly under the influence of things that are happening in the world outside. Recreation, once centered largely in the family circle, has been extended by motion pictures and new forms

of transport to a wide circle of outside influences. Reading materials are available in many parts of the world in such quantities that people sometimes feel that they have less time than before for concentrating on the Bible or books about the Bible. In every country the pace and tempo of modern life have quickened so that even the remoter hamlets are no longer the isolated outposts they were a century or less ago. On top of all this, the international situation presses so hard upon us all that life almost everywhere is marked by less concentration on the affairs of the individual household and more awareness of the unease and restlessness of the world at large.

Still, in these changing circumstances, the Christian home continues to exercise an educational influence. There is today, in fact, in face of all the factors in the outside world that are tending to break up the stability of life, a new tendency to emphasize the importance of religious life in the home. Many realize that the very factors which seem to threaten the centrality of the family are in reality going to make plain once again the truth that nothing in the world can compare with the influence of the Christian home in the fashioning of Christian character. Churchmen in conferences throughout the world frequently address themselves to this question which all Christians need to consider: What can the Christian home do today to supplement, implement, and reinforce the educational work of the church?

In the first place, we must stress that the family is a part of the church. When Christians leave the house of worship, they do not leave the church. If the church has become a reality to them as a fellowship of believers, that fellowship will be remembered every day of their lives, whether they are in contact with their fellow Christians or mingling with others who are not within the fellowship. Just as the first Christians, according to Acts 2:46, met in homes for prayer and the breaking of bread, so the fellowship extends its influence into the homes of church members today. Although the entire congregation may not gather to have distinctively religious ceremonies in each home, whenever the members of a Christian family sit down together at mealtime, they know that they are Christians breaking bread together and not simply members of a household who happen to be having dinner at that particular table. Family members know that just as they remember the absent ones in their prayers, so they are being remembered in the prayers of others in the fellowship. For this reason it is important for the family to say grace together at mealtime. Thus the members of a Christian family remember God, the heavenly Father, who is the Provider of every good and perfect gift, and they remember their oneness with all others in him. This is often expressed in the well-known table grace, "Bless, O Lord, this food to our use and us to thy service, and make us ever mindful of the needs of others; for Christ's sake. Amen."

In some places experiments have been conducted in bringing back common worship to the homes of the people. The sacrament of Holy Communion has been celebrated on dinner tables, the congregation consisting of the members of a family with friends and neighbors invited in for this purpose. In other homes, the Bible is read prior to the evening meal or at breakfast, each member of the family taking turns at reading and offering prayers. The fellowship of the table is a time in which the wider fellowship to which Christians belong comes peculiarly alive with meaning.

The various seasons of the Christian year offer another opportunity for family religious observance. A brief family worship service around the crèche on Christmas eve, or at Epiphany when the Christmas decorations are burned, or early on Easter morning can do much to bring back into family life the meaning of these great festival days in the life of the church's people. Likewise, special remembrance may be marked on anniversaries of marriages, baptisms, confirmations, or deaths. These are all times of special family significance.

It is a great help to the unity of the religious life of the family when each member is aware of the part that each of the others is playing in the life of the family as a whole. When the mother reports to the rest of the family on the meeting of the women of the church, or when the father shows a special interest in the youth group to which the adolescents belong, each member of the family is able to share in the experiences of all the rest in different aspects of the life of the one church.

The principal occasion in the week is the service of worship that takes the family to church to praise God. Possibly the best preparation for Sunday comes on Saturday night when family members remind one another of the next day's significance by laying out their best clothes (a symbolic recognition of the importance of the day of the Lord, though the clothes need not be fine!), by studying for the Sunday church school class which some may be teaching or others attending, and by other means that show that Sunday should be regarded as different from other days, since it is the weekly reminder of the resurrection of the Lord.

One thing that can be cultivated with great profit is a connection between families as families and the religious educational program of the church. Many congregations are stressing family nights at church. These are nights when whole families come to the church for supper and stay for a general program of interest to every age or for separate classes or discussion groups for the different ages. Youth groups often invite their parents to share in round table discussions of problems in which younger people are particularly interested. Sample topics are: "What does the Christian family think about various forms of boy-girl relationships, courtship, and marriage?" Or "How can the difference in the outlooks of the younger and older generations be bridged?" Parents should be encouraged to know as much as possible about the educational curriculum of the church and about any weekday religious classes, so that they can be helpful in referring to these in home conversations or by directly helping the children in their home study.

Mention might also be made of the desirability of having some religious literature available for home use. Many churches publish monthly guides to the reading of the Bible, with chosen passages and explanations for every day in the month. Others put out regular helps to prayer and intercession. Church periodicals of various types are often inexpensive and useful. Parents can often contribute more than they realize to their children's re-

ligious awareness by having in the house not only a Bible
but also some other Christian literature. Because of the
work of various Bible societies, almost anyone anywhere
can today own a Bible, or at least some parts of the
Bible, in his own language and at a price which he can
afford to pay, even though he is poor. But the Bible
should be only the beginning and not the end of Christian literature in the home.

Likewise, homes can be enriched by having in at
least one room of the house some religious picture. Many
of the great painters in the past have chosen themes
from the Bible for their great pictures, and modern artists
are again turning to religious themes. Thus there should
be available reproductions for every taste.

Some people think that the Christian home has ex-
hausted its possibilities as a center for religious education. They are wrong. The Christian home is perhaps on
the threshold of a new era of fresh discovery of the relevance of Christianity to the life of the home. The faith
is lived out in company with others. Nowhere is there
more challenge in the modern world for Christians to
seek to live out their faith in close proximity and co-
operation with others than in the life of the home. The
home is the church on a small scale; it is also the community on a small scale; it can be a most effective teacher
of the art of Christian living both in the church and in
the community.

Epilogue

THIS BOOK BEGAN with the affirmation that the church *has* to teach because of the inward compulsion all Christians should feel to share the gospel of Jesus Christ with all mankind and to help their own people to become adequately rooted and grounded in the faith.

The second chapter showed that the teaching task of the church varies with each national or cultural setting in which the church lives and works, but that the basic task is the same regardless of these peculiarities of place and time.

The third chapter dealt with the relevance of Christian education to those different types of people and age groups which are to be found in almost every congregation. It pointed out that the church fails to fulfill its responsibility unless it ministers to the needs of all within its fellowship.

Chapter 4 treated the wide variety of channels that are used by the church for its diversified educational work; and Chapter 5 was a plea for the use of imagination in teaching, so that various methods might be used to enrich the total teaching ministry of the church.

Chapter 6 called attention to the central place of the teacher, especially the volunteer layman who does his or her teaching in the true spirit of Christian vocation. In the last chapter were outlined some aspects of the life of the Christian home, which, as part of the church, plays a vital role in instructing the young in the real meaning of the Christian life.

It is obvious that these few chapters have only scratched the surface of a very large subject. Yet it is to be hoped that at least some worthwhile questions have been raised in the reader's mind. Perhaps the reader will feel at this point like the student who said at the end of a university course, "Now that we have raised all these interesting questions, what shall we do about working out the answers?" It is precisely this working away at the important questions which constitutes the ongoing task of Christian education. The answers are given to us in the gospel of Jesus Christ. But the educational work of the teaching church is to make the gospel come alive in the person for whose salvation Jesus Christ lived and died and rose again. That church can teach best which is itself taught by its Lord.

Bibliography

Cully, Iris V. *Children in the Church*. The Westminster Press, 1960.

————. *The Dynamics of Christian Education*. The Westminister Press, 1958.

Cully, Kendig Brubaker, ed. *Basic Writings in Christian Education*. The Westminster Press, 1960.

Fuller, Edmund, ed. *The Christian Idea of Education*. Yale University Press, 1957.

Gable, Lee J., ed. *Encyclopedia for Church Group Leaders*. Association Press, 1959.

Grimes, Howard. *The Church Redemptive*. Abingdon Press, 1958.

Henderlite, Rachel. *Forgiveness and Hope*. John Knox Press, 1961.

Miller, Randolph Crump. *The Clue to Christian Education*. Charles Scribner's Sons, 1950.

————. *Christian Nurture and the Church*. Charles Scribner's Sons, 1961.

Schreyer, George M. *Christian Education in Theological Focus*. The Christian Education Press, 1962.

Sherrill, Lewis J. *The Gift of Power*. The Macmillan Co., 1955.

Smart, James D. *The Teaching Ministry of the Church*. The Westminster Press, 1954.

Vieth, Paul H. *The Church School*. The Christian Education Press, 1957.

Wyckoff, D. Campbell. *The Task of Christian Education*. The Westminster Press, 1955.

————. *The Gospel and Christian Education*. The Westminster Press, 1959.